My First Music Book

To order additional copies of this book, contact:
Xlibris
1-888-795-4274
www.Xlibris.com
Orders@Xlibris.com

for Benjamin and Andrew

The Piano Keyboard

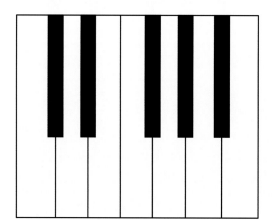

C

do

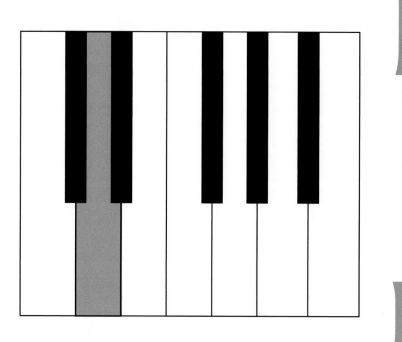

D
re

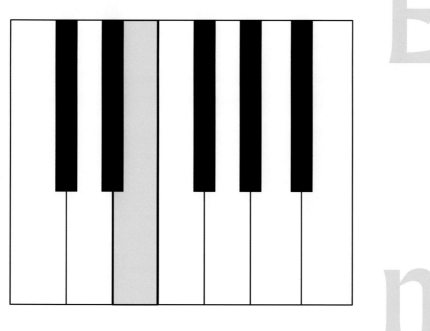

E

mi

F

fa

G

sol

A

la

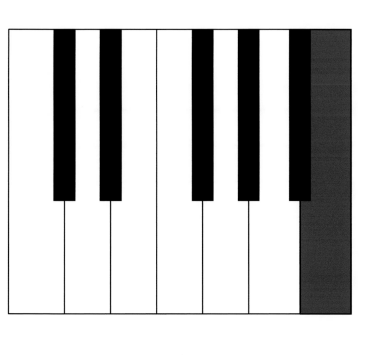

B

ti

Treble Clef

The higher notes

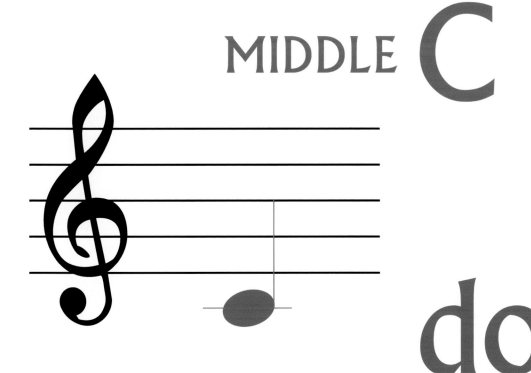

MIDDLE C

do

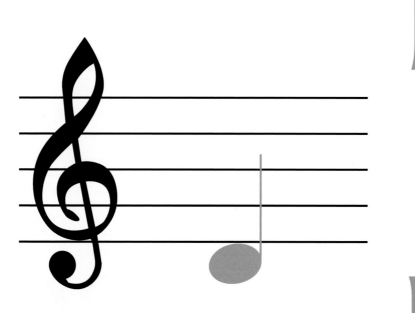

D
re

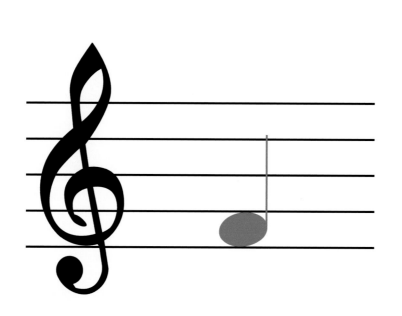

F

fa

G

sol

A

la

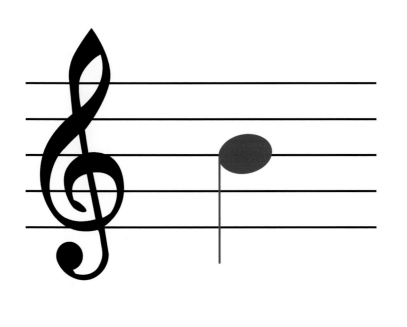

B

ti

Bass Clef

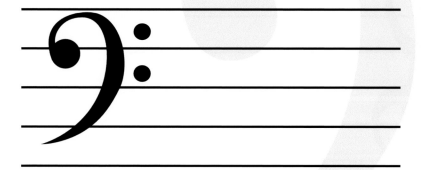

The lower notes

C

do

D

re

E
mi

F

fa

G

sol

A

la

B

ti

Put it all together !

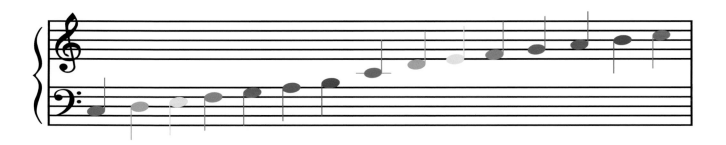

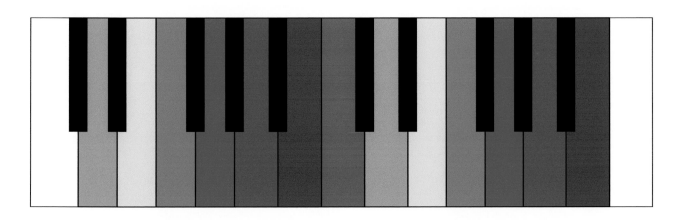

Printed in the United States
By Bookmasters